BEWARE THE
NEUROCOWBOY
A TRUE-ISH STORY OF SALES AND ENTREPRENEURSHIP

Ray C. Rebro

Copyright © 2018 Ray C. Rebro

All rights reserved.

ISBN: 198653166X
ISBN-13: 978-1986531665

DEDICATION

To all those who have worked hard
to make something of value,
and had their ideas stolen by
copycats or wannabes.

Knowledge *is* power.
In the end, you will prevail.

CONTENTS

1	The Day I Asked For Help	7
2	The Day I Got Screwed Over, Again.	15
3	The Day I *Begged* For Help	17
4	The Day Ray Learned 'Neuro'	22
5	The Day Carlos's Way Failed	33
6	The Day My Ego Stood Still	35
7	The Day I Grew Up… A Little	38
8	A Summary of Em's Guidance	41
9	About the Author	44

The Day I Asked For Help

Who am I? You sure you want to know? The story of how I started my business is not for the faint of heart. But let me assure you, this like any story worth telling is all about love—love of money, that is! At least that's how it started.

I remember the cold, windy, overcast day my life began to change, waiting outside Professor Moreno's house. I must have knocked on the door for about ten minutes, but out in the cold it felt like hours.

At last, a crazy, white haired, bushy eyebrowed old man answered the door. He stared at me wide-eyed for a very long time. He smiled a disturbingly slow smile, like the Cheshire Cat —if he had a gold tooth.

"Hello," he said in a gruff, gravelly voice, "I'm the Gatekeeper. Are you the Keymaster?"

"What? No, I'm—." He slammed the door in my face. I knocked again.

"Hello, I'm the Gatekeeper. Are you the Keymaster?"

"Yes! I'm *Vinz Clortho*, Keymaster of *Gozer*. *Volguus Zildrohar* ..."

"Congratulations, you passed the test! Please come in and have a seat."

Ha! Who said *Ghostbusters* trivia was useless?

Inside, I found a dark living room. Was he a hoarder? It smelled like he was, but I saw nothing except for the dusty love-seat I sat on. Could someone like this help me? A twenty-four-year-old business student, and a stinky old man, wrinkly and worn, who had let me into his world on a movie trivia game... two complete strangers sitting across from each other. Where do I start?

"My nam—"

"Don't say a word" he said doing a Doc Brown impression from *Back to the Future*, "I don't want to know your name. I don't want to know anything about you!"

"But—"

"Quiet. Don't tell me anything. I'm gonna read your thoughts! Let's see now... you've come from a great distance, and you want me to buy a subscription to the *Saturday Evening Post*?"

I played along—again. "I'm from the future. I came here in a time machine that you invented. Now, I need your help to get back to the year 1985!"

"Ah, smart boy! Congratulations, you passed the test again. Have a cookie."

A dog biscuit! I saved it for later.

"Okay, who are you and what do you want?" he said dropping whatever game this was.

"Professor Ricardo Emilio Moreno—"

"Call me 'Em'"

"M? Like the Head of the Secret Intelligence Service in the James Bond movies?"

"M for Moreno, 'Em' for Emilio, M like the guy in the Bond films, or like Moriarty in the Sherlock Holmes adventures. Do I need to explain? Call me 'Em'."

"Alright, Em, it's nice to meet you. My name is Ray."

"Ray Stantz?" he asked sitting up.

"Um, no, Raymundo Rebro. I need your help. I'm in this competition for seed money called the *Thunderdome Competition* organized by the Rotterman School of Management and Einsfeynheimer University. I made a project proposal to the teacher organizing the competition, and he helped his favorite student, Carlos, steal the idea from me."

"Sucks to be you," he said settling back into his chair. "Why are you here?"

"This other student, Carlos, he's using *NCC, Neurocommunication Coding*. My aunt, Maggie Martinez— "

"You're Maggie's nephew, huh? I have fond memories of her. Very fond. Very, very fond."

"I...understand. She said you'd help, especially since this guy's stolen my idea about making my pitch using neuroscience, and you're an expert on neuroscience, which is why I'm here."

"Whoa, stop!" he said leaning toward me, "Don't confuse *NCC* with neuroscience! *NCC* was created by Chandler and Tinder in the 70's. Using it is like struggling to keep *Disco* alive after all these decades! Don't worry about it."

"But it's a thing, right?"

"They tried to legitimize it in the U.K. several years ago, but most of it has already been debunked by real science."

"It has the word 'neuro' in it."

"It's neither 'neuro' nor 'science'. Back in the 70's, we knew very little about the brain, okay? NCC took off because its creators looked down on psychology, and they claimed they'd cracked the code to using the brain."

"They looked down on psychology? Down?"

"I know, right? They thought they could do better, but they didn't. Not everything that glitters is gold, and not everything 'neuro' is science."

"Wow! Catchy."

"Thanks. Anyway, if you can't tell the difference then

you'll be wasting a lot of money, and —more expensively— time. Ever heard the saying 'In the land of the blind, the one-eyed man is king?"

"Of course."

"Well, we've been blind about the brain for centuries, and then the 1990's were known as The Decade of the Brain, when new technologies, like fMRI, taught us a lot more."

"Really?"

"But we weren't actually blind, our eyes were merely closed, and we opened them in the 90's when we realized how little we know about the brain. No longer blind to our own ignorance," he said raising his index finger "we embraced it, and eventually disproved many claims about the brain made by so-called experts. As a result, NCC took a serious hit despite some people still peddling it these days."

"Why is it so popular, then?"

"It's not popular among those 'in the know'," he said leaning back. "It's not used or taught in Ivy League Schools or any of the top business schools in Europe, and it's not being researched in any of the sciences. In fact, many big businesses have embraced neuroscience and dropped NCC and never looked back. The investors or judges in your competition," he said shaking his index finger at me," are probably aware and your competitor has in fact made a huge strategic mistake by basing his pitch on NCC. So you don't need my help, kid," he concluded while getting up, "and you'll be fine. Now get out."

"Professor, help me. You're my only hope!"

"I'm not your only hope. There is another…," he said as if he'd said something clever.

"I beg your pardon?"

"It's a reference from The Empire Strikes Back. You do know Star Wars, right?"

"Of course, yes, Rey and Jyn."

"*Rey and Jyn*? No, no—ah, it doesn't matter! I can't help you, this is a waste of time. I'm a researcher, not a teacher! I don't teach because most people are idiots who don't understand what's important."

"Hmm. Most, but not all people?"

"Yeah, not all of 'em. All Homo sapiens come out of childhood scarred but most simply don't learn how to suffer. Suffering's a problem. Won't accept it, much less embrace it and enjoy life on their own terms. I grew tired of them. I don't waste my time on them." In a melodramatic stance, he started quoting Thoreau in an Old-Timey, FDR-like accent, "I wished to live deliberately, I did not wish to live what was not life. Living is so dear, and I wanted to live deep and suck out all the marrow of life. To live so sturdily and Spartan-like as to put to rout all that was not life, to cut a broad swath and shave close, to drive life into a corner, and reduce it to its lowest terms…" And then he looked at me with a stern look and switched to his regular voice, "That's why I became what Albert

Camus calls an Absurd Hero."

"Camoo-who?"

"Philosophy majors do better in business than business majors. Get a frakking clue!"

"Whoa, alright," I said gesturing him to back off with both hands.

"The *absurd hero* embraces the absurdity of life, abandons hope and thereby gains the ability to enjoy each passing moment with passion. That's why I came to be a *Happy Hermit*," he paused a did a Captain Kirk impression, "and why… I…. left everything behind!"

"Hermit? Behind? Your house is a ten-minute walk from the Einsfeynheimer University campus!" I said pointing to the front door. "And…you retired a week ago! If you want to leave everything behind why not go live high up in the mountains and away from civilization?"

"Nine days ago, actually," he said sounding like Brainy Smurf. "If I'd abandoned 'civil-aye-zation' then I couldn't spend my days enjoying life by binge-watching my favorite movies and shows on Webflix! There's no internet in the mountains, dumbass!"

"Hey, feelings… Please!"

"It's a mindset, Ray. You're looking at me like I have a shark head. You don't *have to* understand. Sorry, kid. Besides, you remind me too much of—"

"My aunt? Yourself when you were young?"

"Someone I *really* don't like. Look, read up on Daniel Rock's SCOFF Model. Look it up. You'll do fine."

"Can we be real?" I pleaded trying a Disney movie reference, "If my name was Sebastian and I had a cool Jamaican accent...you'd totally help me. You would. You know you would."

"Ah! You've seen *Moana*, you little snot!", he said with a blissfully goofy grin.

"P—please don't tell anybody! I also cried during *Coco*..."

"Everybody cries when they watch *Coco*, Ray" he reassured with a smile. "*Toy Story 3* was also a tearjer—"

"The thing is," I interrupted, "I have a reputation to maintain!"

His grin vanished. "Oh, yeah? Well, no soup for you!" he boomed. "Get out. Good luck!" he said pointing at the door.

It had been a Hail Mary, but worth a shot. I started my walk back to campus when I heard him call out to me.

"Hey, Ray!" he said standing at the door, "Say 'hi' to your aunt, for me," he said with a Biff-like, devious smirk, and he closed the door.

Dirty, dirty old man! Happy Hermit my ass! Another mad scientist, what a disappointing cliché he turned to be! I can do this without the help of a caricature. I know I can, I know I can, I know I can—Yes. I. Can.

BEWARE THE NEUROCOWBOY

The Day I Got Screwed Over, Again.

The next day, at the campus cafeteria, I was thinking about how I probably won't be able to beat Carlos without Em's help.

What really baked my noodle, though, was wondering if the dog biscuit I'd just ate was stale because I'd saved it, or if was already stale when that old goat gave it to me... Oh, farts! Putting the anxiety aside, I focused on the SCOFF Model, a brain-based framework that helps improve communication.

I was thinking it was a good thing I knew about it, but I'd still need guidance from that nut job on how to use it when, suddenly, Carlos sat down in front of me.

"*'Sup*, loser?"

"Carlos."

"Call me Charles."

"I'm not calling you that."

"How's your project coming along, you big *lew-hoo za-her*? I heard it wasn't such an original idea, you know, compared to mine! You should know I always win, numbnuts. *If you ain't first, you're last!*"

"You think you have an advantage, Carlos, but while you're writing your pitch based on a knock-off of modern science, I'll be basing my pitch on the SCOFF Model."

"SCOFF? Ya don't say? Is that supposed to mean something to me?"

"Yeah, it means you'll be using pop neurobabble from the 70's and I'll be using research-based, proven science. Who's the loser now, *sucka*?"

"I already know the judge's V-A-K preferred sensory channel, loser, so…!" he said jumping to his fee "Scoff *this*!", he gave me the finger and moonwalked away.

He suddenly stopped, hopped to the right and spread his arms out to the sides. He crossed his right foot over his left, hugged his chest, did a 360 counterclockwise, and ended looking to the side. He turned his head to look *right at me*, performed eight hip thrusts while looking straight into my eyes, biting his lower lip. He hopped to the side, raised his right leg with a bent knee, and extended his leg in a snapping motion. He tapped his knee, and returned his right foot to the floor, doing some kind of *Billie Jean* bullshit. He grabbed his crotch, blew me a kiss and walked away.

What the even heck? Ray, you flippin' Urkel, did you just get served? Gosh!

BEWARE THE NEUROCOWBOY

The Day I *Begged* For Help

Next morning, I stood outside Em's house holding an old boom box over my head, blasting *"In Your Eyes"* by Peter Gabriel.

When I want to run away I drive off in my car
But whichever way I go I come back to the place you are...

Em peeked through the curtains and came out the front door. "Who are you, John Cusack?"

I lowered the boom box, and chuckled, "Nah, I'm better off dead!"

"Ah, congratulations, you passed the test once more. Please come inside."

I went inside and sat down, this time noticing the TV. I hadn't been able to see it on my first visit, but everything in the living room was somehow arranged around it. It was almost an altar...

"Professor, I'm trying to find the right words…" I said looking at the floor.

"It is so nice when you can sit with someone and not have to talk." he said extending his pinky like Dr. Evil.

"*When Harry Met Sally*! Good movie! You're really into movies, huh?"

"Movies?" Em touched his chin and looked up. "Neeah…" he said doing a *Bugs Bunny* impression, "Could be!"

"Professor, please help me. The guy I told you about, Carlos, is going to use the SCOFF Model now. He stole another idea from me."

"How the hell did *that* happen?"

"I told him about it. It's my fault. The only way I'll stand a chance now is if you help me out, and I'm going to beg you for help the best way I know how…." I got up, looked him in the eye and with the straightest of faces I said, "*Wubba Lubba Dub-Dub*!"

"What did you just say to me?"

"It means 'I am in great pain, please help me.' It's from *Rick and Morty*."

"I know what it means," he said reflectively. Em stared out the window for nearly a minute. "You know", he said exhaling and shaking his head, "people like Carlos are called 'neurocowboys'."

BEWARE THE NEUROCOWBOY

"Neuro…cowboys?"

"The word *cowboy* refers to a reckless, irresponsible person who undertakes a sensitive or dangerous task. Sometimes they are underqualified to perform it. *Neuro*cowboys don't have any respect for the complexity of the brain nor for the many fields that comprise neuroscience."

"I don't get it."

"They get access to a little bit of information and present themselves as experts right away. They take a course, or read a book or two, and start teaching about the brain, but in Carlos's case he's running with just *one model*… a model he can't possibly fully understand without proper instruction. He's probably going to hurt his credibility in the process."

"But isn't that what you told me to do?"

"What?"

"Didn't you send me off to use a model that I 'couldn't possibly fully understand without proper instruction'?"

"Shazbot! Jebus H. Motherfrakking Cripes! I did, didn't I? I sent you on the way to becoming a *neurocowboy*!"

"Not yet! But I *will* turn into one if you don't help me, Professor."

"Well played, Ray! You made this about *me*! I have skin in the game now, and I *have to* get involved. You've given me a very powerful motivator to not say no: *a good excuse*!

Ha! That's the way, aha-aha I like it!" he sang.

"I've always needed your help to deal with Carlos though, deep down, he's not all bad… We used to hang out. He even came over for dinner once."

"Don't defend him! You've described him like he's a bad hombr—"

"Person!" I interrupted. "Bad *person*. Not really. Not all asshats are evil."

"Yes, well your little friend sounds like a character from an Al Pacino movie."

"His older brother was raised to be an Olympic athlete, eating every hour throughout the day—every day— since before he was ten. Carlos is the underachiever of the family, a victim really. He'll do anything to win the *Thunderdome*. I want to win it fair and square."

"Yes, competitive people often cheat and take shortcuts to win. It's primitive behavior. In '99 a lady with a degree from Haardvark University stole my work, so I sympathize. Also, I can't stand by a let a neurocowboy try to misuse a validated brain-based model, and I can't be the one who turned you into one," he said staring at the floor. "If I help you and guide you, I'd also be getting revenge *vicariously* from the lady who stole my work. Vicariously means experienced through imaginary participation in the life of another person."

"I know what 'vicariously' means." I said, thinking this is how Penny feels like in *The Big Bang Theory*.

"That settles it. *This* will be my revenge! The game's afoot! Come back first thing tomorrow. I'll help you out."

"Thank you, Professor, thank you soooo much!"

"Call me Em. Well, you got what you wanted. There's the door. Get out."

RAY C. REBRO

The Day Ray Learned 'Neuro'

I was back at Em's house early the following day.

"There's the kitchen, Ray. Go in there and make something for us to eat."

"Are you going to 'Miyagi me' and teach me neuroscience while I cook for you?"

"What? No, just frakking make something we can eat while you're here."

I made some scrambled eggs—the only thing I can cook.

"Em, I knew sooner or later you'd come around and help me. I knew this collaboration was destined to be. The universe is conspiring in our favor!"

BEWARE THE NEUROCOWBOY

"Ray, sounds like you watch a lot of Soap Operas. I mean, you are big Paulo Coelho and Deepak Chopra fan, *amairite?*"

"I don't watch Soaps, but Coelho and Chopra are okay in my book."

"I knew it! No, they're *not* frakking okay. There's no fate but what we make for ourselves, there's no such thing as a soul mate, and the universe is most definitely *not* conspiring in anyone's favor!

From monstrous gamma-ray bursts, deadly pulsars, matter-crushing gravitational fields, and matter-hungry black holes, down to tsunamis, hurricanes, or swarms of locusts, and even viruses, parasites, cancers, and congenital diseases… the universe is out to frakking kill us!

Nobody exists on purpose. Nobody belongs anywhere. Everybody's gonna die! Ya feel me, son?"

"Except for the cool *Terminator, Neil deGrasse Tyson* and *Rick and Morty* references, that's just sad."

"It's not sad. Neuroscience is part of biology, the study of living things. The first lesson about neuroscience is that *no one knows everything about the brain.* Okay? No one. Almost 20 major branches of neuroscience don't 'talk' to each other. I'll share the results of my work as a neuroscience researcher for over 35 years, but I don't know everything. Nobody does."

"Got it."

"When this whole *Thunderdome* situation is over, go study someone else's perspective, results, etc. Promise, Ray?"

"Cross my heart!"

"Start with neuroanatomy, okay? The second lesson summarizes my life's work in applied neuroscience: *we're all scared little creatures seeking to be loved.* If you keep it in mind, you'll have better results than if you don't. Is that clear?"

"It sounds catchy, but I don't get it."

"Good, thank you for your honesty. Third lesson is *constantly validate your knowledge.* Few things in life are more dangerous than the illusion of knowledge. Constantly test your hypotheses, and when you don't understand something, go back and test your assumptions. They lead to your understanding or lack thereof. By telling me you don't understand the second lesson when I say we're scared little creatures seeking to be loved, you are following the spirit of this third lesson," he added signaling three the 'German way'—with thumb, index and middle fingers. "Ever heard the phrase 'Stay hungry, stay foolish'? Well, I say *'stay skeptical, stay uncertain'.*"

"You should trademark these phrases."

"Who says I haven't?"

"Fair enough. But if I 'stay uncertain' then, I'll never be sure of anything!"

"Exactly! *That* is what drives scientific exploration!"

"What about everything science can't explain, like the existence of God, and the soul, and all of that?"

"Stay skeptical, stay uncertain, my young friend! Don't hurt others —with actions or words— just because they are sure of their answers and they differ from your answers. Be comfortable with your original opinions and staying undecided for long periods of time. The need for certainty has caused too much suffering inflicted by people who are certain of what hasn't or can't be proven… or at least can't be proven with our current level of understanding and technology. Be *better* than them, Ray! Now, can we get back to your predicament?"

"Yes. Got it, always be in *'learning mode'*. Go ahead, please. Thank you."

"Well put! Now, let's get practical here. These six guidelines or tips helped me with fundraising for my research for years without ever taking a course on marketing or sales. This is why you here. This is it! Are you ready?

"I think so."

"Ahh…, "he said doing a Mr. Miyagi impression," Squeesh just-eh like-eh gu-rape! No mahtteh" and he changed back to his normal voice, "Here we go, the first tip will help understand lesson number two… scared little creatures… what do you think is their biggest concern of all?"

"Sex?"

"Close. I'll give you a hint", he said getting up and doing an exceedingly spastic rendition of a 70's John Travolta dance, which reminded me of *Seinfeld* and Elaine Benes's awkward dance.

"Staying alive?"

"Ahhhhhhhh, ahhhhhh, ahhhhhh, ahhh!" he screeched in an awful, gritty-gravelly imitation of *Bee Gee*'s falsetto. "Yes, all living beings fear death," he said sitting back down. "What to do? *Make them feel safe when talking to you.*"

"How can I do that?"

"Point out, subtly or not so subtly, everything you have in common with them—any similarities between both of you. It can be literally anything you truly have in common. Use empathy! You did it unconsciously by playing along with my movie references and quotes. By the way, that's when I really decided to help you, you know? *All decisions are emotional decisions.*"

"No way! Really?"

"Yeah, you had me at *Jamaican accent*. And then the good excuse helped me not say no."

"You're joking, right? That's what did it? The *Moana* reference?"

"Yes. We're scared little creatures seeking to be loved. It only takes *one thing* to connect emotionally with another person. Doesn't have to be a big deal. Often it's something stupid. But it has to be something makes you think 'this is my kind of guy, or I can be myself around this guy.

BEWARE THE NEUROCOWBOY

Despite the clear differences, you and I shared a love for movies or movie quotes. That did it. I just waited for you to come back, and do a little groveling. Plus, you came and made this about me too. That's how you do it: First create safety and connection, then make it about the other person. If you give them a good excuse not say no, it's even better. It was smart."

"Wow. Not smart, just lucky."

"Starting today, do it *mindfully* —intentionally and on purpose— and make it happen. Do research to create a profile on them: background, achievements, likes and dislikes, etc. Find similarities you can point out. *Be truthful and sincere or you'll destroy trust and scare these poor creatures away.* Help people want to tell you things they were scared to tell you about before… Life is not about rusty trombones, dirty sanchezes, or cincinatti bowties, it's about *connections*", he said intertwining his fingers.

"That reference is from *The 40-Year Old Virgin*!"

"Not bad for non-teacher, huh? Maybe I'm not such a cliché after all."

"How'd you know I thought you were a cliché?"

"Studying the brain is like putting one's empathy on steroids. Blows it up. Kaboom! Anyway…seeking to be loved is important. Is lesson number two a little clearer now?"

"Yes. But what about your *hermit* thing and your need for

connection?"

"Ah! Studying the brain changes you, and I'm out of the popularity contest. Keep in mind I'm a *happy hermit*, not a bitter one—alone in the crowd by choice, and capable of making exceptions also by choice. Enough about me for now, and let's focus on you and your project, alright?"

"Wow. Okay."

"Connection is important, so the truth is your best ally—always. If you like to lie or make up stuff, learn to write fiction and get paid for it. There's an excellent online specialization I can recommend, though I can't quite remember the name... something to do with *Crusher* or *Snipes*, and sounds like the name *Leanne*. In any case, the point is that unless you're writing fiction, stick to the truth!"

"Duly noted."

"Work on a strong person-to-person connection, and tip number two is make everything about them, and make sure that you offer more than what they expect to receive."

"I've heard that before."

"Careful, now! 'I already know this' is the opposite of *learning mode*. These tips work because you use them together. One won't give you an edge. Use the profile and get a sense of what they think is valuable or fair, and exceed their expectations. So far, we have 'create a connection' and 'exceed their expectations', together."

"How do I exceed expectations?"

"You know your product or service —or whatever it is you're proposing, offering or selling. Focus on value and benefits, and always give more than expected. That's practical tip 'two' after creating a connection, but use them together. Tip three is *give them space*."

"Space?"

"Juggle this third ball: When you talk, don't corner them. 'Don't pressure them' is what I'm suggesting. What happens if you put Baby in a corner?"

"She fights back."

"Eh… close enough. Yes, if you corner people they will always fight back. So always, *always* give them space. Connect, exceed expectations, and give them both physical and mental room to move, all three at the same time. *Capisce?*"

"Yes."

"Tip four is: *Don't paraphrase*. You are the only one making an effort to connect and to understand, so make it easy for them to process your message by using *their words*. Listen! Be curious! Get interested in them, and make them talk about their favorite subject: *themselves*. Like you did with me, find a way to make things about them. It's conversational *Judo*. To summarize this tip: don't paraphrase, instead seek to 'parrot-phrase'. So far, we have the first three tips, plus the fourth tip, using their words, not yours."

"Em, you're good!"

"That's what sheeee said!" he sang as I felt my face flush, reminded about my Aunt Maggie...

"Tip five..." he continued, opening his eyes wide to signal he was moving forward. "Did your mom ever tell you it's not okay to compare?"

"Yes, she did."

"Well, the primitive parts of the brain can't process information without comparing. *Always make comparison easy*. Prices, percentages, adjectives, always provide some form of context. If you say, 'our product is better' add context to 'better' or it could mean just about anything. 'Better', can be that it saves 10% more energy compared to your competitors. 'Our product is PABA-free' requires clarifying what PABA is, what its risks are. You can also mention another product and its price to provide context. Think you can use this information?"

"Yes, I can use it in my presentation. Please continue."

"We learn through *analogy* because it makes comparing easy, so the learn to communicate by using stories, anecdotes, and metaphors to convey your ideas. It's a pretty safe bet to rely on stories. Lastly," he added dramatically "tip six is... making everything about them also requires *suspending your ego*!"

"What?"

"This one is the toughest, but one of your most powerful communication strategies. Suspending your ego means: look inside yourself, get to know yourself, find your 'triggers', your emotional 'hot buttons', your issues, your childhood hang-ups, your pet-peeves, your quirks, your personal preferences…. and learn to *put them aside* at least temporarily while you talk to your potential customers. Me?" he said pointing to himself with both thumbs "If I had approached you to talk about fundraising for my lab research, I would have *never* imposed my preferences by joking about movie trivia, and I would have made the whole interaction as Em-free and Ray-focused as possible. Make sense?"

"So, 'suspending my ego' means not talking about my favorite subjects? My preferences are not important?"

"At least not in the beginning, and certainly not if you are pressed for time. Time is precious. Whether spent or invested, you never get it back. Always respect other people's time. Be punctual, be concise, and make the interaction about the other person.

That's it, my young *Padawan*" he said getting up ready to shake my hand. He stood in front of me, wide-eyed as if deciding whether to say something to me or not. "Ray, these are your first steps…", he chuckled and winked, "Three lessons, and six tips is what I have for you given our circumstances and time constraints. Are you ready to go and put all of it into your presentation?"

"Well, I'm certainly ready to try."

"Try, huh? I have a good movie reference for that, but I'll *suspend my ego*…" he smirked.

I stood up, smiling, and shook his hand vigorously. He

offered to help by phone if I needed anything else. As I started my walk back to campus, I heard the front door open behind me.

"Ray, aveeeeeenge me!!" he roared startling everyone out on the street.

A wave of embarrassment moved through me, burning like ignited kerosene. "I will," I replied softly, lazily waving goodbye.

"And, Ray, never cross the streams! Take care now, bye-bye then," he said closing the door.

BEWARE THE NEUROCOWBOY

The Day Carlos's Way Failed

On day one of *Thunderdome*, it was Carlos's turn to talk to the Venture Capitalist judge, Jared Ridley, who would provide funds and mentorship to the winner. Carlos didn't put up any slides, and began his presentation talking in strange-sounding speech patterns, and nodding his head without saying a word. Was he using an NCC trick?

"Hi, I'm Carlos Guerrero, and I have something that will sound like music to your ears! I'm going to offer you a wonderful opportunity to invest in *AI Max*!" he announced while continuing to nod his head.

"Hi," Jared interrupted, "Um, Mr. Guerrero, is your neck... Uh, why are you nodding your head? Is it a trick to get me to agree with what you're saying?"

"Um, no... I don't need tricks, because I'm freaking awesome! Doesn't that *sound* good to you?" he said, still nodding.

"Actually, no. What exactly does your company make? Artificial Intelligence?"

"Yes, but what we make is irrelevant, because you would not be investing in a company or product, but in me."

"Oh? And why should I invest in *you*, Mr. Guerrero?"

"Because it's what a smart person would do."

"Thank you for your time, Mr. Guerrero."

"No, wait. You need to listen…"

"I don't need to do anything, Mr. Guerrero. Times up. Good luck. You're going to need it."

Wow. Painful, but quick. Did he think Jared's preferred V-A-K sensory channel was auditory? I guess Carlos didn't even look over the SCOFF Model! He wasn't using it at all. He didn't make it all about Jared.

I know better than that!

BEWARE THE NEUROCOWBOY

The Day My Ego Stood Still

On day two of *Thunderdome*, when my slides were on the screen and they called my name, before taking my first step on stage, I froze! I could move, but my mind went blank— it had completely stood still!

Over the phone, Em said this might happen, so he taught me the *90 Second Rule*. That's how long changing mental states takes, so if I get angry, panic or freeze, all I had to do was breathe deeply for 90 seconds until the chemicals in my bloodstream were processed. Thank God we'd talked! Fortunately, it took less than 90 seconds, and I walked on stage shortly after being called.

Once there, all my preparation came back to me! I was ready! "Hi Mr. Ridley, I'm Ray, and I want to start by saying I didn't know about you until only a few weeks ago, but I did some research and found it interesting that we both put up lemonade stands in grade school to buy a new bicycle."

"Really? That's cool, Ray. What are you selling these days?"

"Thank you. These days I'm selling a better mouse trap in the form of notchless customizable belts" I said parrot-phrasing and answering in one sentence.

"That doesn't sound new at all."

I was tempted to object, but I forced my ego to stand still. "You're absolutely right, Mr. Ridley, what's new is they also change color to match your shoes or clothes thanks to proprietary technology, and all for $25 dollars or less. That's $10 less than our closest competitor who can't match the color changing feature."

"Match my shoes? Very cool. And please call me Jared."

"Thank you, Jared. We make them for about half that, and a pilot exercise here on campus gave us $4,000 in sales in one week thanks to word of mouth. Over 90% of customer base is male."

"Wow."

As I continued, everything good about my company was presented as a benefit to Jared. Following Em's *other tips*, I used vivid charts, images showcasing the product, happy people wearing the belts, and —to stimulate the most senses possible— I presented Jared with a selection of belts so he could touch and even try them. Em said the whole "one sensory channel preference" thing is a bad strategy, and a true "neuro" approach *engages all senses*. He suggested we have more than five, but left that conversation for another time.

"What's the biggest insight you've had during this competition, Ray?"

"This is embarrassing," I said suspending my ego again, "but at first I thought I was customer-centered, having a great product and all, but I realized I was not actually focusing on people, and their concerns when they buy and try on the belts. So, basically I became less concerned with closing a sale and getting rich, and more aware of the value we can provide during the sales process."

"Interesting."

"Also, the product is great because our teamwork from design and materials to production and logistics gives customers a great price and quicker deliveries."

"Well, sounds like you did some maturing during the competition."

"Yes! 'Maturing' pretty much sums up my experience," I parrot-phrased.

"Well, alright. Thank you for your time. We'll announce the winner in the next few days.

"Thank you, Jared."

Whew! My mind and my ego had both stood still that day.

RAY C. REBRO

The Day I Grew Up… A Little

Three days later, I checked the bulletin board for the *Thunderdome* results, and I'd lost, but I was still smiling! The winner was an entrepreneur selling female apparel—a larger market than the male target niche for belts. As far as my problem getting my ideas stolen by Carlos, I think I did a better job at presenting than he did. While the bad science or ineffective methods may have influenced Carlos's results—the reason he failed—is he's a self-centered asshat.

Em was right, studying the brain changes you. It definitely changed me! If Carlos had studied how the brain works, it may have motivated him to change his arguments and overall sales pitch, but more importantly his attitude and focus, and instead of talking about how great *he* was, the science would have suggested he refocus on the *investor*.

After learning real brain-based insights, I started to try and help people, instead of looking at business and sales as a way to make money. In hindsight, that third day with Em was the day I grew up as a business person.

After checking the bulletin board, before crossing the street from the university campus, I felt a tap on my shoulder. I turned around and it was this tall guy, with shaggy orange-ish hair, and thick eye glasses. He was also a little on the husky side of the Homo sapiens species. No, he was not fat, he was *fluffy*…

"Hey," he said with a huge smile, "I'm Jesse, but people call me 'Buster', and I was in the audience for most of the *Thunderdome*. I caught your presentation and I loved it."

"Yeah? Cool."

"I really liked your product. As you can see, I'm *gravitationally enhanced*, so clearly I'm in your target segment," he said running his thumb between his shirt and his pants, smiling.

"Nah, man, come on!"

"It's okay. I've made my peace with being this way—I'm what you call *notbrad*."

"I'm sorry, you're what?"

"I'm not Brad Pitt." he chuckled and snorted.

"Okay," I said realizing I'd walked straight into that

strange mix of lame and wit.

"I really liked everything you said and your niche product. Jared went with the business with the bigger market share. That's one way to go… I'm a niche guy too, and I was there listening to you thinking 'I like this Ray guy' and well, I want to fund your business. What do you say?"

I froze again—for a brief moment. Maybe more than brief.

"Well? Hellohh? Anybody home?" he asked, "I'd like to fund your project. Are you interested?"

I sighed just a little bit, smiled just a little bit and… with all the vein-popping strength I was capable of, shouted at the top of my lungs the only thing that came to my mind,

"Show me the moneeey!"

It was at that exact moment that I realized quoting movie references is truly and tragically addictive.

BEWARE THE NEUROCOWBOY

A Summary of Em's Guidance

Three quick lessons about neuroscience:

Lesson 1: No one knows everything about the brain. If you want to start learning about the brain, start with basic neuroanatomy.

Lesson 2: We're all scared little creatures seeking to be loved. As oversimplifications go, it's a good description of most basic motivations of Homo sapiens.

Lesson 3: Constantly validate your knowledge. Stay skeptical, stay uncertain... Do not follow any sources of information blindly. *Nullius in verba*...Find your own answers!

Six Tips for Talking to Potential Customers:

Tip 1: People's biggest concern of all is staying alive. They fear death both literally and figuratively (symbolically). Read Ernest Becker's work, if you want to learn more. From a practical perspective, make them feel safe when talking to you. This is important because all decisions are emotional decisions, and they are related to survival. Tell the truth always. It's about connection!

Tip 2: After creating safety and connection (emotions), make it about the other person (more emotions), and give them a good excuse not say no (reason or intellect) so they still have that when the emotions fade away. Do it in that order. Make *everything* about them (read up on *implicit egotism* to take your skills to the next level) , and make sure that you offer more than what they expect to receive. Exceed expectations. Prepare with a profile and do your homework before meeting face to face.

Tip 3: Give them space. When you talk, don't corner them and don't pressure them. Look into the importance of autonomy in Self-Determination Theory for more insights. Connect, exceed expectations, and give them both physical and mental room to move, all three at the same time.

Tip 4: Don't paraphrase. To the extent possible, avoid using new vocabulary they may not know or understand. Don't make them think! Read Daniel Kahneman's *Thinking Fast and Slow* for deeper understanding. Make it easy for them to process your message by using *their exact words* as much as possible. It also clearly shows you are listening to them. In short, don't paraphrase, and seek instead to 'parrot-phrase'.

Tip 5: Always make comparisons easy. Provide context or some frame of reference to make comparing easy. George Lakoff's work on metaphor will provide you with more insights. Use analogy to your advantage when conveying your ideas and information. (stories, anecdotes, metaphors, antithesis, hyperbole, allegory, metonymy, simile etc.). Study Rhetoric, the art of discourse.

Tip 6: Suspend your ego. Look inside yourself, get to know yourself, find your 'triggers', your emotional 'hot buttons', your issues, your childhood hang-ups, your pet-peeves, your quirks, your personal preferences…. and learn to put them aside at least temporarily while you talk to prospects or customers. Don't talk about your favorite subjects or your preferences. Respect other's time. Stephen Walker has a great book called *It's Not All About Me*. Read it!

A bonus seventh tip, mentioned in the story, would be to use as many of these tips at the same time as you can *every time it's your turn to talk* with a potential customer. Think of it as if you were simultaneously juggling different items such as balls, bowling pins or torches. You'll have better results if you do.

Good luck!

ABOUT THE AUTHOR

Ray C. Rebro has studied applied neuroscience for over ten years, and is always in learning mode. He believes not all the answers can be found in neuroscience, and that it is very difficult to study and teach.

Buyer Beware, applying neuroscience is *not* a guaranteed short cut to success in any field. Nevertheless, it can be a big help.

The lessons and guidelines in this fictional short story are *part* of a real persuasion model Rebro has developed over the last eight years.

Even though neuroscience provides major insights into findings from other behavioral sciences, Rebro's model combines neuroscience with theory from behavioral economics and social psychology, and it includes the steps covered in this short story in the recommended sequence.

The model has proven to be amazingly effective!

For feedback and questions, please write to
ray.c.rebro@gmail.com

www.ingramcontent.com/pod-product-compliance
Lightning Source LLC
Chambersburg PA
CBHW070951220526
45471CB00007B/2977